HARVARD

*Manage**Mentor***®

A practical resource for
managers in a hurry.

on

Running a
Meeting

D1514757

HARVARD

ManageMentor®

A practical resource for
managers in a hurry.

on
Running a
Meeting

Harvard Business School Publishing

Boston, Massachusetts

Copyright 2002 Harvard Business School Publishing Corporation
All rights reserved
Printed in the United States of America

Mentor: Nick Morgan
Writer: Nick Morgan
Editor: Sarah B. Campbell
Product Manager: Anne Briggs
Cover Design: Mike Fender
Interior Design: Ralph Fowler
Copyeditor: Lauren C. Howard
Proofreader: Monica Jainschigg
Desktop Production: Yuiko Koizumi
Production Editing: Jennifer Waring
Production Management: Basiliola Cascella-Cheney
Manufacturing: C. Yvonne Hickey

Printed by Goodway Graphics, Burlington, MA.

Requests for permission to use or reproduce material from this book should be directed to permissions@hbsp.harvard.edu, or mailed to Permissions, Harvard Business School Publishing, 60 Harvard Way, Boston, Massachusetts 02163.

ManageMentor® is a registered trademark of Harvard Business School Publishing.

Contents

All about Meetings

Your reason for calling a meeting is based on the objective—
do you need to solve a problem? make a decision? inform a group
about an issue? check on the status of a project?—whatever it is,
the purpose determines the whats, whos, and hows.

How to Prepare for a Meeting

Many meetings fail because of insufficient planning. Keeping
the purpose of your meeting in mind, decide on who should
attend and where and when to hold the meeting, and then build
an agenda that works.

How Groups Reach Decisions

Decision-making meetings take some extra care and preparation.
Even before the discussion begins, everyone involved needs to
understand the decision-making process and how the decision
will be made—whether by majority vote, consensus, or the
leader's decision.

How to Conduct a Meeting

All meetings have the predictable pattern of beginning, middle,
and end. For truly effective meetings, recognize and manage each
element from the opening welcome to getting down to work to
bringing closure and planning for post-meeting action.

When Bad Things Happen to Good Meetings

At times, a meeting can run into problems, and the objectives
are sidelined or even left unfulfilled. But if you are prepared and
ready to handle these problems—most of which are predictable—
you can quickly get your meeting back on track.

Mentor's Message: Why Meet?

Antony and Cleopatra. Lewis and Clark. Ben and Jerry. These are meetings I would like to have attended—at least the first ones. Many business meetings, though, I'm glad to miss. The bottom line? Nobody ever wished one ran longer.

In fact, whenever anyone bothers to study the problem, he discovers two facts: businesspeople spend a lot of time in meetings—anywhere from two-thirds to three-quarters of their workday—and too often they wish it were otherwise.

So why do we spend so much time in meetings? That's where we get together, as teams, as ad hoc groups, as members of a department, as negotiators sitting across from one another at the table. Meetings are where problems are solved, decisions are made, and trust is built.

Okay, then, since we have to meet, let's agree to make meetings as efficient, as useful, as productive—and as *fun*—as we can.

That's what this guide is all about: making meetings worthwhile. And here's what's coming:

- We'll consider when to have a meeting, and when to avoid one.

- We'll work through how to prepare for a meeting, how to run a meeting, and what to do after a meeting.

- We'll talk about the size of meetings, and let you in on a little secret for making sure that your meetings accomplish what they need to: *the 8-18-1800 rule.*

- We'll talk about what happens when good meetings go bad, and what to do about it. The whole point is to equip you for the contest, so that you can jump into the fray ready to transform the meetings you attend.

- We'll even give you sample agendas and various worksheet tools designed to let you get the information you need quickly and easily—perhaps on the way to your next meeting—without having to read too much.

Together, we can make meetings work more effectively than they do now. You won't be able to avoid meetings, but you'll feel better about them.
Let's get to work.

Nick Morgan, Mentor

All about Meetings

The test of a vocation is the love of the drudgery it involves.

—Logan Pearsall Smith

DESPITE EVERYTHING YOU'VE HEARD and witnessed about meetings, they don't have to be boring, needless, and way too long. You can change all that—you can learn how to run meetings right. This Harvard ManageMentor® guide gives you the tools you need to master a critical managerial skill.

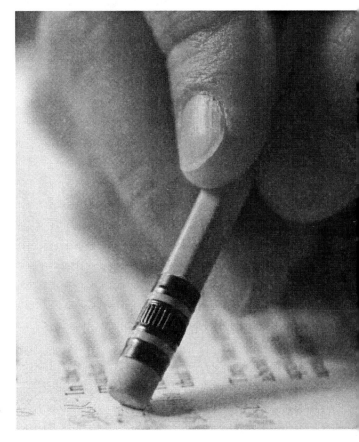

Why have a meeting?

Before you do anything else, figure out what you want to accomplish in a meeting. Decide what you want to get done.

Then, figure out who you need to help you. Once you've got the "what" and "who" down, the rest (when, where) is pretty easy.

You may already have a weekly meeting routine established. Many teams meet on Monday morning to get the group going for the week; others meet on Friday to review the week's activities, progress, and problems.

meeting *n* 1: the act or process of coming together for the purpose of transacting business. 2: an assembly or gathering of people for the purpose of building trust.

In general, call a meeting when you have a good reason to—such as when you:

- need the entire group to provide information or advice on an issue

- want the team to participate in making a decision or solving a problem

- need to clear up an issue that cannot be resolved in a one-on-one exchange

- want to share information, a success, or a concern with the whole group, or make everyone aware of a particular situation

- are dealing with a problem that needs input from members of different groups who have varying perspectives or agendas

- find that responsibility for a problem, issue, or area needs to be clarified

- discover the group feels a strong need to meet

But don't call a meeting when:

- the subject is a personnel issue that is better handled one-on-one

- you don't have time to prepare

What Would YOU Do?

TBIF (Too Bad It's Friday)

IT WAS THURSDAY evening. Maria was dreading her weekly production meeting the next morning. She knew that half the time would be spent as it always was—unraveling problems that had arisen because team members had made ad hoc decisions, putting out small fires without taking the larger blaze into consideration. She could hear the team members already: *"Why didn't you TELL me you were doing that . . . ,"* or *"If I had KNOWN you had made that decision, I wouldn't have gone ahead and . . . "* and the predictable responses: *"I'm sorry, but it didn't seem like a big deal,"* and *"I didn't want to waste everyone's time by calling a meeting."* And it wouldn't be just one or two people raising these issues—it would be everyone!

Maria realized that she needed to help the team communicate more effectively, but how? She had no desire to extend the already grueling weekly meetings, but the alternative—calling a meeting to solve every problem that arose—would be highly disruptive and annoying.

What would YOU do? The mentor will suggest a solution in *What You COULD Do.*

- another method of communication would work as well or better—for example, a memo, e-mail, or telephone call
- the issue has already been decided
- the subject is not worth everyone's time
- the group is upset and needs time apart before being able to address the source of conflict or frustration

Who comes to a meeting?

How many people should you invite?

Let's say you've determined that you do need to meet. Before you think about names of people to invite, decide on numbers.

Here, remember the 8-18-1800 rule:

- If you've got to solve a problem or make a decision, then invite no more than eight people. Having more than eight people in one room always causes more problems than it solves.
- If you want to brainstorm, then you can go as high as 18 people. Just don't look for consensus from those kinds of numbers.
- If you want to disseminate information, send out a memo. Oh, wait, you already decided you had to have a meeting. If you want to whip the group up into a frenzy of enthusiasm for that exciting new product, then the more the merrier. Go for 1800—or more.

Who should come? Easy! Everyone affected directly, up to the limits of the 8-18-1800 rule.

This does mean that you're going to have to make some tough choices at times. Well, that's why you're the manager. Rules are rules. Break them at your peril. Just watch the frustration of a group of 30 people trying to make a decision. They'll remember that you called the meeting, and they won't thank you for it.

Recognize other types of meetings.

We've been talking about standard business meetings, the kind you'll be most likely to deal with. But, of course, there are variations on the themes, and you should be aware of the most common forms.

Exceptions to the rules. The size of the meetings is what defines these exceptions.

- **One-on-one meetings.** These are meetings with your direct reports where you give difficult feedback or talk about next year's raise. And sometimes you'll have to fire someone. Although these may be the most difficult meetings of all, they can't be done honorably any other way than face-to-face. Those stories you hear about people getting fired over voice mail or e-mail? Their managers look bad,

Tip

Remember the golden rule of management: praise in public, criticize in private. That should guide your meeting strategy at all times.

lose trust, and deserve the same treatment.

- **Large corporate meetings.** At the other extreme is a stockholder meeting, during which the CEO reports company activity and results to a large number of stockholders seated in an auditorium. This is really a show, not a meeting. It's entertainment, subject to all the rules of theater. If you get stuck running one of these, get help from a pro. Meetings like this have very little upside potential, and lots of the other kind. People only remember what goes wrong. They don't notice if everything goes smoothly.

Remember the purpose.

In sum, remember that it is the purpose that drives the meeting.

In a **problem-solving** meeting, participants first define a problem and then craft solutions for solving it. Participants in this type of meeting must be able to recognize the problem and also have the energy and expertise to correct it.

In a **decision-making** meeting, the group selects a solution to implement. To be successful, the group must agree on the decision-making process at the very start of the meeting: will decisions be made by *consensus*, by *majority vote*, or by only *one person* or small group? (More on this later.)

All other types of meetings are informational. Seek to cancel as many of these as you can. Mostly, they're a waste of time. Send an e-mail instead. Only hold them when you need the group energy of all those bodies in one room.

Steps for Running a Problem-Solving Meeting

1. Find out what the participants' perceptions of the problem are.
2. Get agreement on the definition of the problem.
3. Discuss how long the problem has been going on and what is happening now.
4. Determine what the group thinks are the causes of this problem.
5. Outline the future consequences of the problem if it is not solved.
6. Brainstorm options for solving the problem. Clarify the advantages and disadvantages of each option.
7. Choose the most effective method for selecting an option. Consider the key factors, such as time, resources, financials, values, and so forth, involved in the choice.
8. Gain full agreement, or at least a consensus, on an option for problem resolution or management.

What You COULD Do.

Let's go back to Maria's meeting dilemma.

The mentor suggests this solution:

Maria realized that she needed to help the team communicate more effectively, but how? She has no desire to extend the already grueling weekly meetings, but to call a meeting as every problem arose would be highly disruptive and annoying.

Here's a suggestion for helping Maria out of her dilemma.

One of the few good reasons to call a meeting is to make a decision. Problems are arising on Maria's team because team members are making ad hoc decisions without consulting the affected people. She may be one of the lucky few that actually needs more meetings. But they needn't take long. If she established a strictly limited, fifteen-minute, end-of-day meeting during which the decisions of the day are aired, she might not need to have that agonizing weekly production meeting.

But there's another option Maria should consider. The essence of the problem is not that people are making decisions, but that the affected people are not learning of those decisions in a timely way. There's not enough intrateam communication. A more disciplined use of e-mail, together with a more tightly controlled weekly production meeting, might solve the problem and make those weekly meetings less painful.

For a thing to remain undone, nothing more is needed than to think it done.

—Baltasar Gracian

How to Prepare for a Meeting

RACIAN IS RIGHT. So don't think you can call a meeting and be done with the preparation! A successful meeting takes thought and planning.

Everything follows from the purpose.

Begin your preparation by identifying the meeting's purpose(s) as specifically as possible. Is it to brainstorm, inform, elicit ideas, fix a problem, determine a course of action, or clarify roles and responsibilities? Your purpose will probably consist of some combination of these reasonable activities. Once you know the purpose, you'll be able to figure out what your objectives are. A *clear statement of purpose and objective* will guide you through the next steps of building the agenda.

Who should attend?

Invite only those who truly need to be there—those people who will allow you to reach your objectives and who will offer a variety of perspectives on the issues. They are:

- the key decision makers for the issues involved
- the ones with information and knowledge about the topics
- people who have a commitment to, or a stake or role in, the issues
- those who need to know about the information you have to report in order to do their jobs
- anyone who will be required to implement any decisions made

How to invite them? Once you've figured out who needs to be there, invite them personally. Make sure they know that you are calling and running the meeting. Let them know what the purpose of the meeting is. Arrange a time for the meeting that works for everyone involved (which can be tough). And try to give each participant an active role to play in the meeting. That way they'll be sure to attend. Businesspeople are paid to be active, not passive. If they have to be passive for long periods of time in a meeting, they get fidgety—and bored.

What about date, time, place, and equipment?

When? If you meet regularly with your staff, the date, time, and place will be part of everyone's routine schedule. If the meeting is a special one, then choose a time that is convenient for all participants.

EXAMPLE: You can send a number of optional times along with your invitation. Or some companies have intranet-based calendars so that you can schedule colleagues based on company-wide information.

Where? The place will depend on the size and purpose of the meeting. Most departments have conference rooms of various sizes to accommodate these group meetings. If you're undertaking some brainstorming, and have the budget, consider going to an offsite location. It's a little more work to arrange, but it usually pays big dividends in the quality of the output.

What? Tables arranged so that participants can see and speak directly to one another promote active dialogue that is best for problem-solving or decision-making situations. Round or U-shaped tables are better if you want to de-emphasize hierarchy. If you want to stress the corporate hierarchy, use rectangular tables with the head honcho seated at the head of the table. Unless the meeting is large and purely informational, auditorium-type spaces should be avoided.

Tip

If you want to make sure that everyone participates, plan to break the group into subgroups for part of the meeting.

Order any equipment you might need prior to the meeting—and test it out beforehand! For any interactive meeting, you'll need a flip chart or white board to record ideas and solutions. You may also need overhead projectors for presentations, speaker-phones to include participants that may be tied in by telephone, and so on.

Build the agenda.

As you go through the meeting-preparation process, use the information you've gained to develop an agenda. Start with the purpose and then the participants.

What goes into an agenda? A typical list of agenda items includes the following:

- the meeting's purpose clearly stated
- the desired outcomes or objectives
- what group is meeting or who the participants are
- the date, time, and place
- the length of the meeting
- who is calling the meeting
- what each participant's role is in the meeting
- each agenda item to be covered (specify the person responsible and the time allotted)
- any background material to be used for preparation

Of course, you can adjust this list to fit your particular situation, such as a special meeting format, or invited guests.

So, you can see that an agenda is a handy list that helps you organize the why, what, who, when, and where of the meeting. Opposite is an example of a typical agenda. In the Tools sections of this guide, you'll find a blank template of this agenda to use as a model for your own meetings.

How long should the list of agenda items be? Include only as many agenda discussion items as the group can realistically cover in the time allocated.

As a general guideline, assume that it will take at least 30 minutes to cover one topic, and two hours to cover five. But remember, the time allocation for your specific issues may vary—some topics you can zip through, others will need extra time for discussion.

Order agenda items carefully.

Sequence of the agenda to create a high-energy flow to the meeting.

First, look for issues that have a logical connection or that build on each other. If you need to make a go/no-go decision about a product launch, for example, don't put next year's marketing plan on the agenda first.

Tip

To avoid last-minute problems and embarrassments, be sure to confirm and check the space, and test any needed equipment ahead of time.

Meeting Agenda

Purpose:	Pricing for New Product
Objectives:	Develop pricing guidelines for new product
Meeting Topic:	To consider the variables that affect pricing; to decide on the pricing guidelines
Attendees:	Tim, Maria, Javier, Ed, Jen
Location:	5th floor conference room
Date and Time:	2:00 p.m., March 20, 200X

Agenda Item	Who	Time Allotted
Opening	Tim	5 minutes
Review of standard product cost, excluding development costs	Ed	5 minutes
Report on optimal distribution channels	Javier and Ed	10 minutes
Review of competitors' pricing	Maria	5 minutes
Report result of customer focus groups, product testing, etc.	Jen	10 minutes
Group discussion of pricing	All	15 minutes
Decide final pricing guidelines	All	5 minutes
Next steps	Tim with input from all	5 minutes

© 2002 Harvard Business School Publishing. All rights reserved.

Tip

Always underestimate rather than overestimate how many issues a group can handle in a given time.

Next, separate the types of issues—share information first, then make decisions, and, finally, solve problems.

If you've got really complicated items on the agenda, break them down into manageable bits.

Leave time for the important stuff, but start with a few easy items to get a nice momentum going. Plan to have the most difficult issues come up for discussion when members are at their clear-headed, creative best. That may mean taking a break for coffee or snacks after some of the work is done, so that you can reconvene with everyone at full energy.

Tip

A meeting without an agenda is like a search party without a map.

EXAMPLE: Start with an easy information-sharing issue, and then work on a difficult issue. The group will be warmed up and attentive.

Assign meeting roles and responsibilities.

As you prepare for a meeting, make sure you've got people covering all the important roles and responsibilities. One individual may fill several roles in a meeting, and if it's *your* meeting, you'll probably wear both the leader and facilitator hats. The essential roles are:

- **Leader.** May or may not run the meeting, but does clarify its purpose, objectives, constraints, and scope of authority. Takes responsibility for follow-up.
- **Facilitator.** Guides the group through the discussion, problem-solving, and decision-making phases of the meeting. May be responsible for pre- and post-meeting logistics.
- **Scribe.** Captures the key points, ideas, and decisions that result from the meeting. May also draft the post-meeting notes. (Notice that I didn't say minutes! More about that later.)
- **Contributor.** Participates actively by offering ideas and helping keep the discussion on track.
- **Expert.** Contributes expert knowledge on particular issues as requested. The expert's contribution to the team may be limited to providing the needed information, unless she is a regular contributor to the team.

NOTE: Carefully define the expert's role and brief her before the meeting about what input you want from her. Let her know about those parts of the meeting in which she will not participate.

Supply other necessary pre-meeting information.

Once you've determined the meeting's purpose and who should

attend, decided on location and duration, assigned roles and responsibilities, and created an agenda, what more can you do to ensure a productive meeting?

Circulate the agenda. Be sure to circulate the agenda, including a statement of the purpose and objectives, a list of expected outcomes, and a suggested amount of time for each issue.

Provide background material. If participants need some background material, collect and distribute relevant documents and data beforehand. This can be especially helpful as it permits everyone to operate from the same body of knowledge—you're more likely as a group to achieve consensus and make actionable decisions.

Encourage participants to read pre-meeting material. But don't count on everyone reading the stuff ahead of time. Remember, not everyone did his homework in high school, either. You can increase the odds that participants will prepare by talking to them beforehand about their opinions and objectives. If you show some interest in their ideas, they'll be more likely to return the favor.

Finally, don't forget the higher-ups. Make sure you brief your manager and other senior managers who won't be at the meeting but who have an interest in its outcome. Provide them with the agenda and other background material, as needed.

Tip If you provide all the participants with enough advance information to bring them up to speed about a topic, you will use meeting time more effectively by avoiding explanations and moving right into an informed discussion.

*Nothing will
ever be
attempted, if
all possible
objections must
be first
overcome.*

—Samuel Johnson

How Groups Reach Decisions

DECISION-MAKING MEETINGS can be tricky. If you are the leader of this kind of meeting, you need to prepare carefully for the event.

Prepare for the decision-making meeting.

If you take time before the meeting to follow these steps, the meeting itself will flow, if not more smoothly, at least more predictably.

• Make sure that all the participants understand that the purpose of the meeting is to make a decision.

• Explain to them exactly what decision-making process will be used.

• Collect and distribute all the expert opinion and background information the group will need to make an informed decision.

• Talk to or e-mail all the participants to encourage them to review the pre-meeting information so that everyone will on the same page at the start of the meeting—or at least you'll have advance warning of those who won't be prepared.

Perhaps the most important part of this pre-meeting preparation is establishing the decision-making process. When you convene the meeting, reiterate at the start how the decision-making will go. You can choose among three ways to come to a decision. Each approach has benefits and drawbacks.

Decide by the majority vote.

Accepting the vote of the majority is a widely accepted, common approach to decision-making.

Advantages:

- Voting by majority generally gives you a decision in a relatively short period of time.

- It's widely perceived to be a fair way to decide things.

Disadvantages:

- In an open vote, people are forced to take a public stand on an issue, which may put them in a win/lose situation.

- The losers often feel their voices have not been heard.

- There may not be complete buy-in to the decision.

Decide through group consensus.

The group consensus method of decision-making is often avoided because of the misunderstanding about the process.

Group consensus means reaching a decision that *everyone* understands, can support, and is willing to help implement. Individual members may still feel that other options are preferable, but **genuine consensus** is established when all members come together around a particular course of action.

EXAMPLE: How do you know when you have a genuine consensus? Comments such as the following can serve as clues.

- "I have my reservations about Option A, but I think it's the best way to go."

- "Option A isn't my first choice, but I do believe it incorporates everyone's needs."

- "I don't think Option A satisfies all our criteria 100%, but I'm prepared to implement it as fully as possible."

Consensus decision-making is advisable in the following circumstances:

- when the necessary change requires complete understanding and buy-in from all parties

- when the decision requires the expertise of an entire group to design or implement
- when the group itself is well versed in the art of consensus decision-making

Advantages:

- A consensus usually results in complete understanding of the decision and its implications by all participants.
- The chance for buy-in from all parties is greatly enhanced.

Disadvantages:

- Consensus is often more difficult to reach, particularly if the group is unfamiliar with the process.
- Consensus usually takes more time than other decision-making approaches.
- Occasionally, no consensus can be reached, effectively stopping progress toward the decision.

NOTE: People are more likely to support a decision that has been reached by consensus. But the process often requires having a fallback position—an alternative in case a consensus cannot be reached within the time constraints. Thus, it's not practical to use consensus decision making for emergencies. Nor does this method work well in situations in which the leader alone is accountable for the result.

The leader makes the decision.

In some ways, decision by the leader is similar to a majority rule because the leader needs to hear what the participants think and is most likely to agree with the majority view.

Advantages:

- This is the fastest approach to decision-making, and when time is short or there is a crisis, it may be the best approach.
- If the meeting participants all understand that the leader is making the decision and why, they are somewhat more likely to buy into the decision than not—if they respect the leader.

Disadvantages:

- Meeting participants may feel that their views have been ignored, particularly if they haven't been given the chance to state their ideas.
- Buy-in of meeting participants is less likely than with the other decision-making approaches.

EXAMPLE: A leader listens to the available evidence and announces his decision to shut down an assembly line because of a recent notification of product contamination. In this case, the leader is responsible for the results of the decision.

Guide the decision-making process.

No matter which type of decision-making process is used, there are some general guidelines that will help make your decision-making meeting effective.

- Even when there is little time, encourage all meeting participants to state their views so that they feel their voices have been heard.

- Restate each view after it is expressed. Begin your summation with words like, "So, what I hear you saying is. . . ." Reflect the view as accurately as you can without criticizing it.

- Try to find the basis for a common understanding, showing the links among the various comments people make.

- Lay the groundwork for implementation after the decision is reached. By setting up action steps and establishing responsibilities, participants will be likely to accept the decision that has been made and the next step of implementation.

Between vague wavering Capability and fixed indubitable Performance, what a difference!

—Thomas Carlyle

How to Conduct a Meeting

REMEMBER, running a meeting is NOT rocket science. Following these simple guidelines will help you avoid some of the most common problems that turn meetings into time-wasters or even nightmares.

Open the meeting with authority.

By taking charge immediately, your meeting can move along smoothly. The initial purpose, questions, and clearly-stated procedures will set the right tone for a successful event.

Begin the meeting on time. Even if a few participants are missing, start the meeting as though they were there. When they arrive and discover they have missed some important points, they'll know not to be late next time. Don't back up and start again, or you will only reward the latecomers.

Introduce the matters to be discussed. Hold a brief introductory discussion to make sure the group is clear about the agenda, objectives, and desired outcomes of the meeting—then make any necessary adjustments.

Establish or review the ground rules.
That is, the behaviors and principles group members agree on to ensure a constructive meeting. Here's a list of some basic ground rules:

- Commit to beginning and ending on time.

- Agree about who may contribute to the agenda.

- Understand how decisions will be made.

- Set a time limit on solving each problem or making each decision. Get approval from the group before going beyond the time allotted to a particular topic.

- Clarify constraints that exist for any issue—for example, upper-management decisions or policy or budget constraints that may limit the group's range of options.

- Identify the final decision maker for each item.

- Ask for *everyone's participation* and openness to new ideas.

- Agree to listen to each other and limit interruptions.

You can probably think of other ground rules, but if you at least have these items covered, you'll be okay.

Run the meeting skillfully.

Here are the basic guidelines. Get these elements mastered, and you'll be a meeting pro!

Follow the agenda. This is the prime directive. You've put all that prep work in on the agenda and on making sure the meeting will be a success. So once you're actually rolling, don't be drawn off to non-agenda topics. Stay on track as much as possible. If you stray from the agenda path, you'll quickly lose your focus. And you'll earn the ire of almost everyone else in the room.

Remember, it's a good idea to begin with the easy matters: a brief report or a simple decision to be made. This will smooth the path for the more difficult topics to come. When you're in the midst of discussion, keep an eye on the issue and the time—or assign a timekeeper. Decide when the group has come to an agreement on a topic, recognize it for all, and then move on. Don't let things get sloppy.

Make sure all points of view are heard. As the leader, you want to hear everyone's thoughts. Otherwise, you'll have angry participants after the meeting who will tell you—or, even worse, tell someone else—that they felt left out. So, ask for feedback regularly—at each natural break in the meeting, or at least after each agenda item.

Tip

If participants don't know one another, take some time for personal introductions. This should include name, department, role in meeting, and so on.

For a small meeting, your agenda can be relatively loose, but for a larger group, the more structure you provide, the more effective the meeting will be.

There are several ways to accomplish getting feedback:

- Ask a general question, such as, *"Have we forgotten anything?"*

- Let the quiet ones have a chance to speak up. Or call on them directly.

- If you've got a meeting with more than about ten people in it, break the group down into pairs or trios, and have each small group report back.

- Give the group a little time to think things over. Don't be in a rush to vote or reach a decision.

- If all else fails, ask someone to play devil's advocate to stir up debate.

Don't forget that you called the meeting and thought hard about who should be attending. So don't you want to give everyone a chance to speak?

NOTE: All points of view are valuable, but, in reality, they don't all carry the same weight, and you need to recognize this fact. For example, a senior manager may get the meeting started by stating the purpose and objectives. Then, you might ask the senior member to wait to give his or her opinion on the matter until everyone else has spoken.

Keep the meeting focused. Even as you solicit everyone's opinion, it's important to keep the meeting focused on the tasks at hand. You can

do this by summarizing and reviewing the progress of the meeting frequently. Record the ideas expressed under certain topics on a flip chart. Highlight the transitions from one agenda item or objective to the next. And pause periodically to tell the group where they've been, where they are, and where they're going. All of these actions can work well to keep the group focused.

Be aware of yourself as the leader. You need to be aware of yourself as leader and the responsibilities that go with leadership every moment. The way you act as leader and facilitator creates an environment that encourages people to contribute and keep the discussion on track.

Here are some points to keep in mind as you conduct a meeting:

- Monitor your own level of participation to make sure you're not dominating the discussion.

- Make it possible for quiet or shy people to contribute—control interrupters and dominators.

- Be positive and encouraging about the things people say.

- Praise is a simple and effective way of keeping participants happy.

- Intervene if a participant criticizes or attacks another member's contributions.

In addition, remember to highlight areas of agreement—write

them on a flip chart or white board for all to see. This record of agreed-upon points reinforces what the group has in common and prevents the group from reverting to issues that have already been settled.

When you sense intense interest in a particular issue, watch and listen for everyone who wants to contribute. Acknowledge these people with eye contact or a nod, or by saying, *"Let's hear from Sue first, then Rob, and then Alicia."*

Does all this sound like a lot? It's not really—it's mostly common courtesy and a few tricks of the trade.

NOTE: Recording comments on a flip chart or white board demonstrates to group members that their input is valued. It also helps you keep track of key points and decisions. Some suggestions:

- Keep the comments you've recorded visible for the entire meeting.

- During a brainstorming session, capture every contribution. Then number, star, circle, or otherwise mark up the pages as the group evaluates, prioritizes, and makes decisions about the ideas generated.

- Keep a separate list—sometimes referred to as a "parking lot"—of issues to be dealt with after the meeting.

Tips for Getting Full Participation

- Monitor your own level of contribution to ensure you do not dominate the discussion.
- Be positive and encouraging about the things people say.
- Record everyone's input on a flip chart.
- When you sense there's a lot of interest in discussing a point, start watching and listening for everyone who wants to contribute. Then acknowledge them with eye contact and a nod or by saying, *"Let's hear from Rob first, then Sue, then Tonio."*
- To get input from everyone, go around the room asking for each person's input. But remember that this can be a time-consuming activity, so use it only for important matters.
- Watch for body language signals. If a person is leaning forward, that may mean he wants to contribute. Go ahead and ask, *"Phil, do you have a point to make?"*
- Call on those who have not contributed, if appropriate.
- Remember that silence doesn't always mean that a person is not participating. Be sensitive to a person's need to listen.
- Break the group into pairs or trios and have each group report back.
- Don't rush to vote or make a decision before you've heard all points of view.

Provide closure at the end.

Beginnings and endings are often ignored or considered lesser parts of the event. Not so! For almost any type of meeting, the beginning sets the tone and the conclusion makes the purpose of the meeting actually happen.

Summarize the meeting. This phase brings the meeting to a close. Either the leader or a participant can perform this function. Be sure to reiterate key points, decisions, and next steps, along with who is responsible for what task. This process brings together loose ends and clarifies any misunderstandings. It's also a good time for brief motivational message.

Record the highlights of the meeting. Make sure that you have a scribe writing the important stuff down: the key agenda items, the major discussion points, the decisions made, and the agreed-upon responsibilities after the meeting, together with who has them and how long they have to get them done.

You don't need minutes, unless they are a legal requirement. What you need is a one-page summary. Let's be real about this. No one has the time or inclination to read minutes any more, but they do need to know the key action items during and after the meeting.

Pat yourself on the back—you've done it! And it gets easier as you become more experienced!

Meeting Phases and Tasks

Think of every meeting as having three distinct phases: opening, work, and closing. Each phase has its own characteristic tasks, accomplished by the leader and/or meeting participants. Consult the chart on the following page to trigger your own thoughts about what tasks are appropriate to the meeting you are planning.

Tip

Every group meeting goes through three phases:

1. an opening up (or warming up)

2. a work phase during which tasks are accomplished

3. a closing phase when the matter of the meeting is summarized and next steps are determined

Meeting Phase	Tasks

OPENING

Set the stage for the meeting and get the group oriented, warmed up, and ready to start work.

- Welcome participants; introduce new members.
- Review the meeting's purpose and its expected outcomes. (Answers the question: *"Why are we here?"*)
- Review the agenda. Solicit input, if appropriate.
- Gain agreement from members on the purpose or agenda.
- Establish or review ground rules, if appropriate, such as asking people to speak only for themselves, listen to others, approach the task with an open mind, and so forth. Ask for agreement or commitment, if appropriate. (Answers the question: *"How will we work together?"*)
- Review key roles and who's doing what, including facilitator and note-taker or scribe.
- Gain agreement, if appropriate, on how decisions will be made and what authority the group has.
- Point out use of a "parking lot" board to keep track of issues that may arise that are important but external to the meeting itself.
- Review housekeeping details, if necessary, especially in longer meetings: timing and breaks, access to bathroom facilities, use of cell phones, and so on.

WORK

Actively work on the tasks and issues of the meeting.

- Follow the agenda; work on accomplishing the meeting's objectives.
- Facilitate discussion and decision making.
- Manage or resolve conflicts.
- Use the "parking lot" to keep track of items outside the purpose of the meeting. Assign someone to be the point person for each item.
- Discourage interruptions and unacceptable behavior. Review agreed-upon group norms if appropriate.
- Monitor time as the meeting proceeds. If remaining tasks exceed the time left, solicit input from the group on how best to use the remaining time or present options for how the remaining issues will be handled. Don't just run out of time.
- Change the group structure to help accomplish tasks and get people involved; for example, divide a *(continued)*

Meeting Phase	Tasks
WORK *(continued)*	larger group into smaller subgroups that break off to work on items, then report back to the whole group.
	• Have the scribe or note-taker record issues discussed, key points or decisions made, and other details.
	• Use a flip chart to record and highlight information for the group.
	• Facilitate participation and keep the channels of communication open.
CLOSING	
Bring the meeting to a clear, constructive close.	• Summarize the progress of the meeting.
	• Review major decisions and/or agreements and commitments made.
	• Gain closure on issues if possible. If not, develop a way for outstanding issues to be addressed, such as in a follow-up meeting or by an ad hoc subgroup.
	• Develop next steps, with input from the group. Assign a person to be responsible for each step and establish a rough timeline, if possible.
	• Ask for feedback on how the group worked, if appropriate.
	• Ask if there are any outstanding questions or comments that need to be expressed, and answer them or refer the person to someone who can answer them.
	• Wrap up any loose ends, if possible.
	• Offer some feedback to the participants and a closing motivational message, if appropriate. Thank participants for their contributions.
	• Restate next-meeting logistics if available: when and where the next meeting will be, if an agenda will be sent out, and so forth.

When Bad Things Happen to Good Meetings

The most immutable barrier in nature is between one man's thoughts and another's.

—William James

Be realistic.

You've been planning a meeting for weeks, down to the smallest detail, and you wonder, "*What could possibly go wrong?*" Unfortunately, even if you've followed all the guidelines for conducting an effective meeting, things can still go wrong.

So, what kinds of bad things might happen? Well, here are few typical examples:

- People who arrive late or leave early

- Participants who whisper and disturb the meeting either intentionally or just because they feel like whispering

What Would YOU Do?

Grand Central Station

GALIB HAD JUST COME BACK from another meeting that seemed to be taking place in a train station instead of a conference room. Completely frustrated, he wrote down the agenda they had actually followed—it certainly wasn't the one he had distributed!

AGENDA

Meeting to Determine Phase 2 Problems and Action Items for Project Sarcco
Monday, May 12 , 10:00 a.m.–12:30 a.m.
Fishbowl Conference Room

10:00–10:15	Tom and Cathy show up, chat, have coffee.
10:15–10:20	Sue, Greg, and Jill arrive, discuss the new chairs in the lobby.
10:20–11:05	José enters and we start (even though Bill, who asked to be invited, still hasn't arrived). We discuss four major issues, make decisions, and begin to generate action steps for the first issue.
11:05	José remembers he has another meeting, and leaves.
11:07–11:10	Bill arrives, leaves to find coffee cup, and returns.
11:10–11:20	Bill (who has not read agenda and has not read reports distributed to the team since the last meeting) listens to a summary of discussion that went on during the previous 45 minutes.
11:20–11:30	Bill raises objections to two of the four decisions, reminds us of the project vision, and exits. Cathy leaves.
11:32–11:40	Sue, Greg, Jill, Tom, and I discuss what to do next.
11:40–11:50	Jill and I clean up coffee cups, wipe off table.

Galib knew that he needed to do something to make these meetings more productive, but could he really force people, especially his superiors, to show up on time and stick to the agenda?

What would YOU do?

- One participant who dominates the meeting and infuriates everyone else

- A group that gets stuck or confused, focusing on only one small part of the issue at hand or repeating the same point over and over

- A group that runs out of energy or simply falls silent

- A group that commandeers the meeting and focuses on an off-agenda item

- Members of the group who disagree to the point of breaking—shouting, storming out, and leaving ill feeling in the air. (But this doesn't happen very often!)

Be Prepared!

All these things—and more—can happen. The best way to handle problems is to prepare for them as much as possible ahead of time. How to prepare? Watch for signs of typical problems emerging and then intervene as needed.

Use active listening and observation.
Listen to the emotions underneath the words a participant is saying. What is the person describing? How is the person feeling? Where in her remarks does she place emphasis or energy? What grabs and holds her interest or attention?

Also listen to the language. What kinds of words, metaphors, or images does the person use? If she's talking in terms of war metaphors, that may indicate how she sees, or "frames" the issue in her mind.

You can often read a person's feelings best through body language. If a participant leans forward, interrupts frequently, or gestures a lot, that may indicate passion. Or, if she keeps her arms folded across her chest and sinks back into the chair, she may feel disengaged.

Depending on the results of your observations, the following intervention techniques can serve as first-aid measures to help you get a group back on track.

Be ready to act!

You may not be able to predict all the bad things that could happen, but there are some general patterns of meeting flow and participant behavior to watch for. If you are prepared for them, then you'll be ready to act as soon as necessary. Rescuing a meeting can be a very satisfying experience.

If some participants arrive late or leave early:

- Consistently begin and end meetings on time.

- Give participants (especially those who have a habit of being late) a job to do during the meeting.

- At the beginning of the meeting, ask the group if everyone can stay until the designated end time. If not, consider adjusting the length of the meeting.
- After the meeting and in private, ask the person why he missed part of the meeting. Find out what the underlying causes for the behavior may be, if possible.

If a participant dominates the discussion:

- If you are standing, walk closer and closer to the person. This tends to draw group attention *to* you and *away* from the speaker.
- Thank him for his input, and call on someone else.
- If he finishes other people's sentences, encourage him to let other people speak for themselves.
- Ask the group to change roles so that the quiet people speak up and those who have been talking remain silent for a while.
- For chronic interrupters, during a break, ask them to jot down their thoughts and wait until there is a pause to contribute them instead of just shouting them out.

If the group keeps repeating points already made:

- Keep track of ideas on a flip chart or white board.

- Be sure to confirm your understanding of the ideas presented by "active listening." That means restating ideas by saying something like "*What I hear you saying is . . .*" and repeating back to the participant a fair and accurate summary of what he said.
- When someone begins to repeat an already listed idea, point to the chart or board and ask something like, "*It looks as though we've already covered that point. Is there something new you want to add?*"
- If people still keep coming back to the point, you can seek resolution on the spot, saying something like, "*Well, this is obviously important to the group, so let's deal with it right now.*"

If some participants disturb the meeting:

- Explain the ground rules for participant behavior at the beginning.
- Try asking a question, being sure to include the transgressors among the people you'd like to hear from.
- Try asking for a single focus, saying something such as "*Our purpose today was to shape our innovation strategy for the year. Can we please focus on that again?*"
- Call for a break if the problem continues. Then, during the break, ask people individually what's going on. Get at the reasons for the

Tact is the art of making a point without making an enemy.

—Howard W. Newton

disturbance and, if necessary, directly request the offending parties to stop. Tell them you'll address any legitimate concerns after the meeting.

EXAMPLE: Interrupters can be especially frustrating. When Chris interrupts Leslie, you need to say to Leslie, *"Take your time, Leslie,"* and to Chris, the interrupter, *"Please let Leslie finish."*

If the group gets stuck on or confused about an agenda item:

- Don't ignore the problem.

- Ask the group what's going on.

- Remind the group where it is on the agenda and what the specific objectives are. Point to the flip chart or the white board if you've been working with one.

- Remove the obstacle, if possible. See if the group is stuck because it lacks sufficient information or clarity about the task or about how to proceed. Ask the group if there is a key point or issue that has not been raised and needs to be.

- Suggest a short break if none of those attempts works. Then, return to the topic at hand or move it to a later position on the agenda or to another meeting.

- Remove the item from the agenda if all else fails. Remember the words of Scarlett O'Hara, *"Tomorrow is another day!"*

If the group falls silent:

- Let it be silent for a minute. Wait before giving them a suggestion. The group may need time to reflect upon an idea or what they're feeling about an issue.

- Check out what's happening, what people are thinking. You can ask the group directly, *"I notice that you've fallen silent. Can someone say what's happening here?"*

- Ask people if they would like you to clarify something.

- Ask them if you are unaware of a key point or issue or if you have caused some confusion.

- Think about whether *your* behavior might be the problem. Ask yourself if you came on too strongly in an opinion or a preconceived solution.

- Take a short break to refocus and find new energy.

- If the group just seems worn out, consider ending the meeting and rescheduling.

If there's a hippopotamus in the room:

If the group is avoiding an issue or focusing on one issue to the exclusion of others, it may be because members are afraid to bring up a particular subject. We call this problem "The Hippopotamus in the Room"—meaning that there is a big, obvious problem everyone knows

Tip

There are many ways of energizing a weary group. Throw a beach ball around; stand up and do some stretches; tell some jokes; have a snack.

about but no one wants to mention. If that's the case, it's your job to face the hippo directly and then move the group on.

NOTE: There may be topics, however, that seem too difficult or even "forbidden" to raise. For example, if participants know that an increase in funding would easily solve a problem, but that the resource limits are binding, they may feel frustrated. Or they may be concerned about an impending round of layoffs, so they won't be at their best in a group meeting.

How to face the hippopotamus:

In most cases, it's enough just to raise the issue to get the group moving again. Nonetheless, you need to ask contributors to be precise about the nature of problem, issue, or opportunity. Then find out how long it has existed, who is involved, and what the consequences are. And remember to thank a participant if he brings up a controversial or different viewpoint. That way, you'll reinforce the idea that constructive debate is often a good way to find solutions.

Let the group know how important it is to bring up all options, concerns, and issues, even if they are difficult. Let them know you will not "kill the messenger." It's a common

human urge to blame the bearer of bad news, but it's wrong, so don't do it. And once you promise not to, keep your promise or you will lose credibility and trust.

If real, angry conflict arises:

- Call an immediate halt to any bickering. If necessary, take a break and speak to the contenders individually.

- Let all members know that it's fine to be passionate, but ask people who are unable to control their tempers to deal with their issues outside the meeting room.

- Reaffirm the norms for behavior that have been agreed upon.

- Focus on the substance of ideas or opinions—not on the contributor's personal style or status in the organization.

- Encourage members to keep their comments positive and constructive and to try to see all sides of a contentious issue.

- Keep members from evaluating ideas too quickly. For example, when some participants seem to be touchy about each other's suggestions, one thing you can say is, *"Now there's an idea. Let's not evaluate it just yet. Just let me write it down now, and we'll get reactions to it later."*

What You COULD Do.

Let's go back to Galib's meeting dilemma.

The mentor suggests this solution:

Galib knew that he had to do something to make these meetings more productive, but could he really force people, especially his superiors, to show up on time and stick to the agenda?

The quick answer to Galib's dilemma is: YES! You *can* force (or at least nudge) people, especially your superiors, to show up on time and stick to the agenda. In fact, that's one of the most important jobs of the person in charge of the meeting.

Galib's company has a real problem in its corporate culture. That kind of sloppiness—which wastes everyone's time in the long run—develops gradually over time. To change that kind of culture takes a firm hand.

First, Galib should enlist the aid of the highest-ranking person in the meeting to help enforce discipline. This is a time to get the supervisors involved as participants. A little enforcement is what's needed.

Next, Galib should send out a memo with his next agenda, explaining that problems with meetings are leading to inefficiencies. Thus, he's going to take some steps to modify the culture. He might conclude his message with these words, *"Meetings will start and end on time and stick to the action items on the agenda. If you come late or leave early, your voice may not be heard in the discussion or decisions being made."*

Most importantly, Galib needs to follow through himself by starting the meeting on time and ending it on time.

- Use probing questions to steer members away from entrenched positions and to help uncover the underlying issues.
- As a last resort, ask the contenders to leave the meeting.

Practice wearing other hats.

The implication behind the intervention techniques discussed here is that there are additional roles—beyond the essential ones of leader and facilitator described earlier—that a leader must be prepared to fill in the course of a meeting. Depending on the dynamics at work within the group, the leader sometimes has to perform the duties of

- **Gatekeeper.** Ensure that the agenda is followed, that everyone who wants to speak gets the opportunity, and that no one person dominates the discussion

- **Devil's advocate.** Challenge a consensus that may be emerging prematurely, that is, without sufficient thought

- **Consensus builder.** Spot and highlight areas of agreement among members

- **Cheerleader.** Give praise to members where it is due (as honestly as possible)

- **Joker.** Relieve tension and remind members of common bonds. Use humor to relieve tension, but don't make jokes that exclude some members or that come at others' expense.

- **Boomerang.** Return a question to the person who asked it. This sends the message that the leader is not solely responsible for answering all questions.

How to Handle End Matters

No grand idea was ever born in a conference, but a lot of foolish ideas have died there.

—F. Scott Fitzgerald

KNOWING WHEN, AND HOW, to end a meeting—and what to do afterwards—can help you galvanize team members to carry out the agreed-upon plan of action.

End the meeting on time.

By concluding at the promised time, you keep the trust and gain the appreciation of all participants. If you're the sort who has trouble ending things on time, try these tactics:

- Ask a group member to be a time-keeper.

- Periodically remind the group of the time remaining and the agenda items they have left to cover.

- Prioritize or postpone some agenda items if time is running out.

- If more time is needed, gain the group's agreement to run overtime, or schedule another meeting to deal with the still-pending matters.

End the meeting early, if possible.

No one ever protests when you end a meeting early. In fact, there are a few situations where it's best to end early.

- If you've got everything done, don't stay in the room just to fill out the allotted time. That's bizarre and annoying in this time-deprived culture. Instead, send everyone on their way.

- If the group is having trouble with the last item of business, this may be a sign of waning attention or energy. It's a good idea in that case to agree to finish that item at another time.

- If your people are getting restless, that's another sign that energy and attention is running down, and it's best to honor the body language and cut things short. You won't be likely to get much more done anyway—certainly nothing much of quality.

- If the discussion is heated or acrimonious, a quick end to allow for cool-down may be the best option.

Provide closure.

So, you've concluded that it's time to end. Is there anything special you need to do? Basically, just give everyone a sense of closure.

1. Restate and summarize very briefly what's been accomplished.

2. Clarify what comes next—action items, who's responsible, the communication plan, relevant dates, and the like.

3. Schedule another meeting, if necessary.

4. Ask the group for an evaluation of the meeting, if there's time. If not, tell them you'll canvass them later by e-mail or in paper form—or informally, if the group is small.

5. Finally, thank everyone for participating.

You're done, right?
Almost. Now comes the follow-up.

How to Follow Up after a Meeting

Sometimes in life, situations develop that only the half-crazy can get out of.

—François, duc de La Rochefoucauld

THE MOST OVERLOOKED PART of running a successful meeting is good follow-up. Following up energetically is the single most important thing you can do to make the meeting (and any to follow) a success. Meetings that end without a communication and action plan often have no life outside the meeting room. After all, the point is rarely the meeting itself, but rather the action that comes out of it.

Ensure post-meeting success.

What are some of the ways you can influence what happens after the meeting? First, communicate with all the participants and other stakeholders with an e-mail or memo that both summarizes the meeting and points to next steps (not the minutes, which few people read). Then, take time to talk with participants who seemed unhappy with the meeting—they'll appreciate your attention. Also, make sure to provide the par-

ticipants with the resources they'll need to accomplish their individual post-meeting tasks. Most important of all, act! Don't let things slow down and get lost. Act on the decisions made and keep the spirit going.

Develop a communication and action plan.

A communication and action plan provides both closure and a sense of accomplishment. It also alerts all stakeholders to key decisions and helps to ensure that all have heard the same message or information. A communication and action plan should have three elements—what, who, and when:

- **What** specific decisions and outcomes resulted from the meeting, and what tasks need to be done as a result of the meeting?

- **Who** has responsibility for these tasks? If meeting participants have voluntarily committed to undertake specific actions during the meeting in front of other participants, it's more likely they will complete those tasks.

- **When** must the tasks be completed? Keeping participants realistic about the schedules they commit

What Would YOU Do?

Did We Have a Meeting?

LAST WEEK, Judy ran a great meeting. She had invited the right people, communicated the goals clearly, and distributed clearly written background reports and agendas beforehand. She listened carefully, kept things on track, but was flexible enough to accommodate some unexpected ideas that arose. She moved the group toward consensus. They arrived at a thoughtful decision and created a strategy that was realistic and inventive.

There was only one problem. Since the meeting, no one had talked about the decision or the strategy at all. Everyone continued to pursue the projects and priorities they had been working on prior to the meeting. Even Judy was beginning to wonder if the meeting had ever even happened.

What would YOU do?

to helps ensure that tasks actually get carried out.

What goes into a communication and action plan? Detail what was accomplished in the meeting, based on the points recorded on the flip chart or white board and the notes you or the scribe took during the meeting. It needs to be written so that someone who wasn't there can understand what happened. The plan covers

- attendees
- meeting objectives
- key topics discussed
- key decisions made
- next steps or action plan
- date of next meeting or follow-up
- a thank-you to those who participated

For specific types of meetings, the communication and action plan may have more specific items. For example, the communication and action plan for a problem-solving meeting might include more specific information:

- the definition of the problem
- the method of analysis
- the alternatives discussed
- the criteria for deciding
- the decision
- who follows up by when
- the expected outcome

If at all possible, fit the information on one page.

There's an example on the following page. You'll find a blank version of this communication and action plan in the Tools section of this guide.

Send the communication and action plan out to all stakeholders. Fine-tune the communication and action plan, and then send it out in the form of a follow-up memo to all meeting participants. Also send the memo to people who were not at the meeting but need to be informed.

Listen to the dissatisfied.

Don't forget to meet informally later with those who seemed dissatisfied. You may notice that some participants appeared to be unhappy with the results of the meeting or didn't contribute as much as others. Follow up with these people. You may learn something valuable, such as helpful feedback about the meeting process, agenda topics, objectives, and action plans. You will also probably soothe an unhappy colleague and improve overall group relations.

Evaluate the meeting.

I'll close with the Big Question. How do you know if your meeting was effective?

Judge by the results. Did you accomplish your objective(s)? Were

> Tip
>
> Communication and action plans are more likely to be carried out if they are viewed as actual responsibilities, obligations, or contracts.

Communication and Action Plan

Start filling out this form in your meeting to keep track of the issues discussed and the decisions made in the meeting. After the meeting, fine-tune the form and then send it out to all meeting participants and other people interested in the results of the meeting.

Meeting Topic:	New Product Launch
Attendees:	Anne, Pedro, DC, Gabe
Purpose:	Check progress of Product X and Product Z
Objectives:	Ensure process is on critical path
Agenda Item #1:	Product X status
Options/Points Raised:	Legal review; Quality control
Decision or Recommendations:	Prepare for test market
Agenda Item #2:	Product Z status
Options/Points Raised:	Product testing; Sales rollout
Decision or Recommendations:	Delay sales rollout by 1 week
Agenda Item #3:	
Options/Points Raised:	
Decision or Recommendations:	

Action Items

Task to Be Done	Person Responsible	Due Date
Report from Legal	Gabe	2/1
Test market prep	Anne	2/10
Retest Product Z	DC	2/4

© 2002 Harvard Business School Publishing. All rights reserved.

the right people there—did they show up? Did most people participate? Did the group work effectively together? Were the evaluations positive?

If you've done a good job, you'll find yourself answering "Yes" to most of these questions. If that's the case, a quiet celebration is in order. Getting a meeting to go right is not easy.

What You COULD Do.

Remember Judy's problem?

The mentor suggests this solution:

Since the meeting, no one had talked about the decision or the strategy at all. Everyone continued to pursue the same projects and priorities as they had been working on prior to the meeting. Even Judy was beginning to wonder if the meeting had ever even happened.

The seeds of Judy's problem began during that apparently great meeting. She did everything right except the most important thing: the follow-up. It's the job of the meeting convener to insist on clear action items during the meeting, together with assignments for each item and follow-up measures. Who's going to do what, with whose help, by when? That's what Judy needed to know and what she failed to establish.

After the meeting, it's your job as the meeting leader to write up a brief one-pager that summarizes the key decisions, actions steps, responsible parties, and schedule for follow-through. That summary should be sent out to everyone affected, including people in the meeting and people who weren't necessarily there.

If that one-pager shows clear responsibilities, dates and names, then it will be easy for Judy—or you—to ensure that the next steps are taken. But if she hasn't established responsibility during the meeting, no one will feel obligated to act on what was decided, and the meeting will become The Meeting That Never Was.

*He would like
to start from
scratch. Where
is scratch?*

—Elias Canetti

Virtual Meetings

THE OLD, FAMILIAR MODEL for a business meeting with everyone sitting around a table is changing. With advances in telecommunications and participants dispersed around the globe, virtual meetings are becoming a familiar model for meetings today and in the future.

Learn to run new-age meetings.

The best meetings are face-to-face. Indeed, if highly contentious matters are at stake, or if the topics are emotional or sensitive in nature, face-to-face meetings are the only ones that will do.

However, the reality of the business world today is that people are no longer working in the same building, city, or even continent. As a result, more and more meetings are virtual in nature; that is, the participants meet via technology—speaker phones, video-conferencing, and so on.

By and large, the same rules apply

to these virtual meetings as apply to face-to-face ones. Special tips for some newer media follow.

Videoconferencing. The current state of the art is still primitive. You'll probably find a videoconference less satisfying than you think it should be. That's because most people compare the technology to television, where the quality of the production values (if not the scripts!) is very high. Professional lighting and sound make television look and sound good, but they are noticeably lacking in most videoconferencing set-ups. The result is a fatiguing and amateur-looking experience.

Also, videoconferences are best used when the parties have already met and established trust—but not for initial meetings. During an initial meeting, the inevitable awkward moments caused by the technology may get blamed on the other participant!

That said, videoconferences do allow particpants to see each other. They can be a useful, timesaving way to tie together remote team members for regular meetings.

Audioconferences with Internet support. We're all familiar and comfortable with the telephone, so if you have to tie remote participants together and you need to exchange some visual material or data in real time, an audioconference with Inter-

net support can be a great alternative to videoconferencing.

If you do have lots of data to exchange, ensure that all parties have high-speed Internet connections, or else frustrating delays will keep some participants out of the loop. Test the connections thoroughly beforehand, and offer a quick tutorial to everyone at the beginning of the call if the software or Web site is unfamiliar to some.

Webconferencing. This term covers a wide range of possibilities, from simple slide sharing on a Web site to full streaming video. In general, the more bandwidth required, and the more complicated the transmission that's being attempted, the more likely that it won't work very well. Test the technology extensively beforehand, and opt for the simplest possible connection.

Chat rooms and other live Web connections. A number of businesses are experimenting with instant messaging and chat rooms as ways to enable far-flung teams to communicate instantly. This kind of arrangement is fine for casual chats and quick questions, but not for formal meetings. Chat rooms by their very nature lead to overlapping typed "conversations," and these, while often entertaining, are not very useful in a business setting.

Tools for
Running a Meeting

Meeting Planner's Checklist

Use this checklist to be sure that you have covered all the important steps in preparing for an effective meeting.

Have You...	Yes	No	Notes
1. Identified the purpose of the meeting?			
2. Identified the objectives of the meeting?			
3. Selected the participants and identified roles?			
4. Identified the decision-making process (for example, group leader, majority vote, consensus)?			
5. Decided where and when to hold the meeting and confirmed availability of the space?			
6. Identified and confirmed availability of any needed equipment?			
7. Notified participants of when and where?			
8. Developed a preliminary agenda with purpose and objectives clearly stated?			
9. Sent the preliminary agenda to key participants and other stakeholders to sound them out in advance?			
10. Finalized the agenda and distributed it to all participants?			
11. Sent any reports or items needing preparation to participants?			
12. Verified that all key people will attend?			
13. Prepared yourself (for example, handouts, overheads, and so on)?			

© 2002 Harvard Business School Publishing. All rights reserved.

Meeting Agenda

Purpose:	

Objectives:

Meeting Topic:

Attendees:

Location:

Date and Time:

Agenda Item	Who	Time Allotted

© 2002 Harvard Business School Publishing. All rights reserved.

Communication and Action Plan

Start filling out this form in your meeting to keep track of the issues discussed and the decisions made in the meeting. After the meeting, fine-tune the form and then send it out to all meeting participants and other people interested in the results of the meeting.

Meeting Topic:	
Attendees:	
Purpose:	
Objectives:	
Agenda Item #1:	
Options/Points Raised:	
Decision or Recommendations:	
Agenda Item #2:	
Options/Points Raised:	
Decision or Recommendations:	
Agenda Item #3:	
Options/Points Raised:	
Decision or Recommendations:	

Action Items

Task to Be Done	Person Responsible	Due Date

© 2002 Harvard Business School Publishing. All rights reserved.

Test Yourself

Test Yourself offers 10 multiple choice questions to help you identify your baseline knowledge of *Running a Meeting*.

    Answers to the questions are given at the end of the test.

1. Everyone agrees that it's important to keep a meeting as short as possible to achieve the meeting's objectives. To be more precise, what is the suggested reasonable time range to consider for a small group business meeting?

  a. Thirty minutes to no more than three hours
     (with at least one break if over an hour).

  b. As short as possible with a maximum of four hours
     (with a break, if over two hours).

  c. Plan on 30 minutes to two hours.

2. As you create a meeting agenda, you have an opportunity to sequence the items for discussion. Which one of the following is NOT a suggested way to sequence meeting discussion topics?

  a. Sequencing from easy to most controversial or complex issues.

  b. Separating information-sharing from problem-solving items.

  c. Going from most controversial to least controversial
     (to allow enough time).

3. Suggested tips for opening a meeting are beginning on time, going over the agenda topics and meeting objectives (and adjusting them if need be), and then reviewing or setting "ground rules" for the meeting. What are ground rules?

  a. The informal votes taken (in a small group) to limit the agenda items to those agreed on in the previous meeting and to keep the meeting short.

  b. The behaviors and principles the group members agree on to ensure a constructive meeting.

c. Roberts' Rules for conducting a meeting; group members agree to using Roberts' Rules or to selecting a different set.

4. In many meetings, a wide range of ideas and opinions may be expressed. What is the suggested strategy for keeping track of ideas expressed and decisions made during a meeting?

a. Record the key points on one or more flip charts or a white board, and keep them visible for the entire meeting.

b. Have the meeting note-taker take notes and track the discussion; ask him or her to summarize as needed, then send out the minutes as soon as possible after the meeting.

5. Imagine you are conducting a meeting around a topic that you know is controversial. For some reason, only one point of view about the topic has been raised. You know there are other perspectives and that they need to be heard. Which one of the following is NOT a suggested strategy to elicit different points of view?

a. Ask someone to play devil's advocate.

b. Call on those who have not contributed.

c. Break the group into pairs or trios and have each group report back.

d. Note aloud that there are other perspectives the group needs to consider before voting; describe the other perspectives yourself.

6. When it's time to make a decision, a group can vote or reach consensus, or the leader may make the decision. Though each approach has its pros and cons, many of us are wary of having the meeting leader make the decision. What are the pros of having the leader make the decision?

a. Leader decisions can take the least amount of time; the important thing to remember is that all members need to feel their viewpoints have been heard.

b. When the leader makes the decision, no individual or faction in the group wins or loses; the important thing to remember is that leader decisions may not build consensus.

c. When the leader makes the decision for the group, the preceding discussion helps identify who is on board and who is not; a key thing to remember is that the leader should not announce any decision until all perspectives have been heard.

7. Constructive conflict can be a key to getting the best answers. However, personality clashes and bickering are definitely not constructive. To encourage productive debate and discussion, you need to reinforce positive guidelines. Which one of these reinforcers is NOT a way to encourage constructive discussions?

   a. Emphasizing that people should bring up contentious viewpoints and that they are important.

   b. Stating that if you, as leader, believe the discussion has gotten personal, you have the authority to tell the involved parties to leave.

   c. Emphasizing that people should not make negative, personal, or unprofessional comments about others.

8. Meetings that end without a communication and action plan often produce no action outside the meeting room. What are the three elements of a communication and action plan that are required to ensure effective follow-up?

   a. What/why specific decisions were made, including the supporting ideas. Who has assumed responsibility for following up on the decision. How each task is to be completed.

   b. Where/when decisions were made, including dates and decision makers. What tasks have been generated related to each decision. Who assumed responsibility for each task.

   c. What specific decisions were made and what follow-up is required. Who is responsible for each task. When each task is to be completed.

9. Who should receive the communication and action plan?

   a. All meeting participants.

   b. All who attended and any other stakeholders who were not present.

   c. All stakeholders who were not present at the meeting. The plan summarizes the key points and decisions made at the meeting; you may or may not decide to send it to the meeting participants since they already know what went on during the meeting.

10. Knowing when to end a meeting can be as important as knowing how to prepare for or conduct one. Which one of these alternatives is NOT a suggested time to end a meeting?

a. End when the objectives are achieved.

b. End when progress toward meeting the objectives ceases.

c. End when time is up.

d. End when any key decision maker must leave, even if time is not up yet.

Answers to test questions.

1, c. Plan on 30 minutes to no more than two hours for a small group business meeting.

Tell the participants before the meeting how long the meeting is planned for and then review the planned length at the meeting again and seek understanding of the time commitment.

2, c. When planning your meeting agenda, moving from most controversial to least controversial is NOT recommended. The more effective methods of sequencing agenda items are to move from easy to the most controversial or complex issues, separate information-sharing from problem-solving items, and plan to have items build on one another.

3, b. The ground rules are the behaviors and principles the group members agree on to ensure a constructive meeting.

These could include setting a limit on discussion time for each topic, agreeing on ways to handle conflicts of ideas or opinions, or making a commitment to begin and end on time. Clarifying the ground rules at the beginning of a meeting frees the members to focus on the topics and may avoid misunderstandings.

4, a. Recording key points or issues on a flip chart or white board and keeping them visible during the entire meeting creates a focal point for the members and ensures that each individual agrees with what's there. It also minimizes the tendency to repeat points that have already been made.

5, d. Giving the other perspectives yourself is NOT one of the suggested ways to elicit all points of view.

One or more of the other options will generate other perspectives. Most important, don't rush to vote or make a decision just because discussion seems to have ceased.

6, a. If it's understood that the leader will be making the decision and why, leader decisions can take the least amount of time.

Leader decisions are frequently appropriate for emergency situations or situations where the leader is accountable for the decision. However, in leader decision making, it's important that all members feel that their viewpoints have been heard.

7, b. While it's appropriate to remind the group that if two people are unable to control their tempers, they may may be asked to deal with their opinions outside of the meeting room, you do NOT, as leader, want to impose the kind of authority that tells anyone at the meeting to leave. That's a misuse of authority among colleagues.

8, c. A communication and action plan should contain three elements: what, who, and when. A plan including all three provides closure and a sense of accomplishment. It also ensures that all stakeholders are aware of the decision or information and helps to ensure that everyone has heard the same information.

It's a fact: Action plans are more likely to be carried out if they are viewed as actual responsibilities, obligations, or contracts.

9, b. Everyone involved in the issues discussed and decisions made during the meeting should receive information about the conclusions and resolutions of the meeting. This includes both the meeting participants and any other stakeholders.

10, d. When a key decision maker must leave is NOT one of the suggested times to end a meeting.

The cues for when to end a meeting are when the objectives are achieved, when progress toward meeting them ceases, or when the time is up!

To Learn More

Notes and Articles

Karen Carney. "Making Meetings Work." *Harvard Management Update*, October 1999.

> Some meetings are effective; others are a dismal waste of time. In this article, use five tips to get the most of all your meetings. Includes box titled "We have to stop meeting like this."

Alison Davis and Kristi Droppers. "How Effective a Facilitator Are You?" *Harvard Management Communication Letter*, January 2000.

> This self-assessment quiz debunks some popular myths about effective meeting facilitation. The best meetings occur in a nonhierarchical setting in which people are able to speak freely, and the conversation is guided but not tightly controlled. Includes a sidebar entitled "Five tips to help you become a more effective facilitator."

Harvard Business School Publishing. "Coping with Conflict." *Harvard Management Communication Letter*, November 2000.

> Conflict in meetings is often unavoidable. In the worst case, it can derail the meeting and stop progress in its tracks. But when conflict is managed well, it can actually improve the process. The key is knowing both how and when to intervene. Includes a sidebar entitled "Landmines," which describes different types of destructive individual and group behaviors and how to address each.

Michael Hattersley. "Managing Meeting Participation." *Harvard Management Communication Letter*, February 1999.

> Most managers spend a great deal of their time in meetings. But are they all necessary? Begin by asking yourself what your personal goal is for the meeting, what—if any—hidden agendas there may be, and what the takeaway from the meeting should be. This article also offers tips on how

to make the best use of your time by figuring which meetings are vital, and which could be replaced by other forms of communication.

Tom Krattenmaker. "Before and After the Meeting." *Harvard Management Communication Letter*, October 2000.

Meetings are the kudzu of corporate life. They quickly cover everything, and nothing kills them. Can you think of a meeting that you wish had run longer? Fortunately, there is a way to make meetings work better. It requires thinking about meetings as a process that starts well in advance of the actual meeting and continues long after it's over.

Paul D. Lovett. "Meetings That Work: Plans Bosses Can Approve." *Harvard Business Review* OnPoint Enhanced Edition. Boston: Harvard Business School Publishing, 2000.

You've got a great idea—now how do you present it in a planning meeting so that your boss approves it? Too many managers overload a plan presentation with unimportant facts or supply inadequate information. To get your boss's approval, ensure that your presentation answers these four questions: (1) What's the plan? (2) Why do you recommend it? (3) What are your goals? (4) How much will it cost?

Nick Morgan. "The Effective Meeting: A Checklist for Success." *Harvard Management Communication Letter*, March 2001.

Meetings have become a popular target of corporate jokes, too often viewed simply as napping opportunities. But "productive meeting" doesn't have to be an oxymoron. Following this checklist can help you make sure that your meetings generate accolades and useful output—instead of yawns and muttered curses. Includes a sidebar entitled "Give Your Standing Meetings a Makeover," which offers specific tips for improving your regularly occurring meetings.

Books

Michael Doyle and David Strauss. *How to Make Meetings Work.* New York: Berkeley Publishing Group, 1993.

Doyle and Strauss emphasize the use of a facilitator as a neutral meeting leader and the value of consensus for improving the quality of decision making. They cover the universal basics of running meetings as well as special points about handling group and interpersonal dynamics.

Harvard Business School Publishing. *The Manager's Guide to Effective Meetings*. Harvard Management Communication Letter Collection. Boston: Harvard Business School Publishing, 2001.

This comprehensive *Harvard Management Communication Letter* resource collection contains 10 articles on how to run effective meetings.

Charlie Hawkins. *First Aid for Meetings: Quick Fixes and Major Repairs for Running Effective Meetings.* Newberg, OR: Bookpartners, 1997.

A complete reference guide to running meetings on purpose, on time, and for results. Offers common-sense advice along with uncommon wisdom. Strategies, tips, and tools will help you improve the planning and effectiveness of your meetings.

Frances A. Micale. *Not Another Meeting! A Practical Guide for Facilitating Effective Meetings.* Ceantral Point, OR: Oasis Press, 1999.

Transform ineffective meetings into productive ones with these guidelines for creating agendas, preparing for meetings, and beginning and ending meetings skillfully. Includes advice for handling difficult situations—such as chronic late arrivals and lack of ability to reach consensus.

Robert B. Nelson and Peter Economy. *Better Business Meetings.* Chicago: Irwin Professional Publishers, 1994.

With the pace of work and the rate of change moving ever faster, managers need to spend considerable amounts of time in meetings sharing information and making decisions. They also need tools and techniques to make those meetings productive and engaging. This book explains strategies and tactics to help make meetings a useful management tool rather than a waste of time.

Gerry Spruell. *More Productive Meetings.* Info-Line Series. Alexandria, VA: American Society for Training & Development, 1997.

This booklet describes the different purposes of meetings and the common characteristics of effective meetings. Contains advice for planning and conducting more efficient, productive meetings. Covers the special roles participants play and ways to deal with difficult people. Includes a meeting-planner checklist.

Sources for *Running a Meeting*

We would like to acknowledge the sources that aided in developing this topic.

Nick Morgan as subject matter expert and mentor, 2001.

Michael Doyle and David Strauss. *How to Make Meetings Work.* New York: Berkeley Publishing Group, 1993.

Michael Hattersley. "Checklist for Conducting a Perfect Meeting." Harvard Management Update, July 1996.

Nick Morgan. "The Effective Meeting: A Checklist for Success." Harvard Management Communication Letter, March 1, 2001.

Robert B. Nelson and Peter Economy. *Better Business Meetings.* Chicago: Irwin Professional Publishers, 1994.

James P. Ware. "How to Run a Meeting." Harvard Business School Case Note, July 7, 1986.

Notes

Need smart, actionable management advice?

Look no further than your desktop.

Harvard ManageMentor®, a popular online performance support tool from Harvard Business School Publishing, brings how-to guidance and advice to your desktop, ready when you need it, on a host of issues critical to your work.

Heading up a new team? Resolving a conflict between employees? Preparing a make-or-break presentation for a client? Setting next year's budget? Harvard ManageMentor®Online delivers answers and advice on 33 topics right to your desktop—any time, all the time, just in time.

- Downloadable modules on 28 essential topics allow you to build a personal management resource center right on your computer

- Practical tips, tools, checklists, and resources help you enhance productivity and performance now

- Advice from seasoned experts in finance, communications, teamwork, coaching and more—accessible with a few mouse clicks

- Multiple language versions available

Go to **http://www.harvardmanagementor.com/demo** today to try out two complimentary Harvard ManageMentor® (HMM) Online topics.

Individual topic modules are available for $14.95 each, or you can order the complete HMM Online program (33 topics in all) for $129. Corporate site licenses are also available. For more information or to order, call 800.795.5200 (outside the U.S. and Canada: 617.783.7888) or visit www.havardmanagementor.com/demo.

HARVARD
Manage Mentor®
An online resource for
managers in a hurry